W9-CRR-134

Why did God invent golf?
(See page 3)

What do you call a black millionaire physicist?
(page 15)

What would Princess Grace be doing if she were alive today?
(page 84)

What do you get when you cross a Chinaman and a hooker?
(page 4)

What do cowboy hats and hemorrhoids have in common?
(page 103)

How can you tell when you're in a gay church?
(page 72)

Truly Tasteless Jokes Two

* **Blanche Knott** *

BALLANTINE BOOKS · NEW YORK

Library of Congress Catalog Card Number: 83-90018

ISBN: 0-345-32921-X

Manufactured in the United States of America

First Edition: July 1983
Twentieth Printing: April 1985

To my mother-in-law

Since I owe the entire contents of this book to the generosity of friends, what could be more tasteless than to acknowledge only a few of them: Gary, Peter, Bridget, Michelle, Matthew, Betty, Neil, and especially Marilyn.

Contents

Ethnic Jokes —Variegated

Why do Italian men have mustaches?
    So they can look like their mothers.

What's Irish and comes out in the springtime?
    Patio furniture.
    (Paddy O'Furniture... get it?)

Did you hear about the advertisement for Italian army rifles?
    "Never been shot and only dropped once."

What do you get when you cross a Pole and a Chicano?
    A kid who spray-paints his name on chain-link fences.

What are the first three words a Puerto Rican child learns?
    "Attention K-Mart shoppers..."

Two guys are walking along, and Harry keeps going on about how he hates Italians. "Greasy wops," he grumbles, "always makin' noise. And talk about *dumb*.... Wish they'd go back where they came from."

In the middle of this harangue, they come to a street corner where there's an organ grinder. He really looks the part: one earring, tattered gypsy jacket, and is loudly singing "O Sole Mio." So Phil is astonished when Harry digs a $1 bill out of his pocket and gives it to the organ grinder's little monkey.

"What'd you do that for?" he asks. "I thought you *hated* Italians."

"I do," sighs Harry, "but they're so cute when they're young."

Why do Puerto Ricans throw away their garbage in clear plastic bags?

So Italians can go window shopping.

A black, an Irishman, and an Italian are trying out for a TV quiz show. The emcee explains that all they have to do is complete the sentence and spell the word they come up with. All three candidates nod in understanding. The announcer's voice booms out the first question: "Old MacDonald had a———"

"Farm," says the Italian. "F...a...r...m...e."

"I'm sorry," says the announcer. "Right word, wrong spelling. Next, please: Old MacDonald had a———"

"House," says the Irishman. "H...o...u...s...e."

"So sorry," says the announcer. "Wrong word, right spelling. Next, please: Old MacDonald had a————"

"Farm!" says the black. "E...i...e...i...o."

Why did God invent golf?

    So that white people could dress up like black people.

A Jew and an Irishman are having a lofty discussion about sex, the Irishman maintaining that it's work and the Jew that it's pleasure. Unable to come to an agreement, they agree to discuss it further at another date.

At their next meeting, the Irishman announces triumphantly that he had checked with his priest. "He says it's work, purely for the purpose of procreation, you see?"

The Jew is far from satisfied, and goes to talk the matter over with his rabbi. Reporting on his findings to the Irishman, the Jew says, "My rabbi says it must be pleasure, because if it was work we'd have the blacks do it."

What's the difference between an Italian grandmother and an elephant?

    Fifty pounds and a black dress.

3

What do you call a Mexican with a vasectomy?
    A dry Martinez.

How do you solve the Puerto Rican problem?
    Tell the blacks they taste like fried chicken.

What do you get when you cross a Chinaman and a hooker?
    Someone who'll suck your laundry.

A four-passenger plane is halfway across the Pacific when it becomes obvious that it's having serious engine troubles. Eventually the captain comes over the PA system to make a grave announcement. "Passengers," he says grimly, "I'm afraid that with our current load, this plane is never going to make it to land. In fact, the only way any of us are going to make it, since there's no cargo aboard, is by jettisoning passengers. Now since I'm the captain, I've got to stay put, but I'm sure we've got three gentlemen aboard who will sacrifice themselves for the greater good."

"*Vive la France!*" exclaims a young Frenchman and, clutching his beret, opens the emergency hatch and plummets out of sight.

After a slight pause, a stout British man stands up. "Long live the Queen!" he says proudly, making for the door.

There was a long pause, following which a big Texan stands up. Grabbing the hapless Mexican sitting next to him, he tosses him out of the hatch, shouting, "Remember the Alamo!"

During a strategic battle of World War II, a Jew, a black, and an Irishman had the misfortune to be blown to smithereens by the same shell. And so they found themselves at the gates of heaven, where St. Peter greeted the Irishman first. "My boy," he said, "it's obvious to me that you've been fighting on the side of Good and Justice, and to reward you, I'm giving you a second chance at life on earth. Get along now."

Rather unable to believe his good fortune, the Irishman stumbled into the bivouac to report to his commanding officer. "My God, man," stammered the incredulous officer, "how'd you get back here...and what happened to your companions?"

"Well, sir," explained the soldier, "St. Peter let me back to earth for free, and when I left the Jew was trying to get St. Pete down from $100 to $19.99, and the black was trying to get someone to co-sign a loan."

On a transatlantic run a freighter came across three survivors of a shipwreck, bobbing about, sunburned and thirsty, in a rubber raft. The freighter's captain, a Britisher, leaned over the side and shouted, "I'd like to rescue you fellows, but I've a few questions first." Of the first man, a hardy Welshman, he asked, "What was the worst disaster in naval history?"

"That would be the sinking of the *Titanic*," replied the Welshman, and the captain threw down a rope and pulled him up.

The next question he posed to the Irishman: "Can you tell me how many died?"

"I'd say about 1250 people," came the reply, and a rope was dropped over the side to pull him aboard.

"You're from Australia, aren't you?" said the captain to the lone man in the raft, turning away from the rail. "Name 'em."

How do they say "fuck you" in Los Angeles?
    "Trust me."

What's black and white and red all over?
    An interracial couple in an automobile accident.

Did you hear that Alitalia and El Al were merging to form a new airline?
    It's going to be called Well I'll Tell Ya...

This little Jewish guy, couldn't weigh more than seventy pounds, goes to Houston on business. He checks into the hotel, which is fifty stories high, and is shown into a suite the size of a ballroom. Overwhelmed, he goes down to the bar and is served a glass it takes him both hands to lift. "Everything's big in Texas, pal," says the bartender with a wink.

When his steak dinner arrives, the plate can't even be seen. "Hey, everything's big in Texas," says the waiter.

Finally, overcome by all of this, the little guy decides it's time to hit his super-king-size bed, only to lose his way in the hotel's vast corridors. Opening the door of a darkened room, he falls into the swimming pool with a great splash—and surfaces to shriek, "Don't flush!"

Did you hear about the Italian engineer who invented a car so energy-efficient it didn't need any gas at all?

It's called the Ronzoni Downhill.

Or about the Italian driver in the Indianapolis 500 who had to make seven pit stops...to ask directions?

How do you get forty Haitians in a shoebox?

Tell 'em it floats.

What's an innuendo?

An Italian suppository.

Why do Mexicans drive low-riders?
So they can cruise and pick lettuce at the same time.

What did the Mexican do with his first 50-cent piece?
Married her.

Why don't Mexicans have barbecues?
The beans fall through the grill.

How many cigars does it take to kill ten Mexicans?
Juan Corona.

In America, they say, "It's 10:00—do you know where your children are?"

In England, they say, "It's 10:00—do you know where your wife is?"

In France, they say, "It's 10:00—do you know where your husband is?"

In Poland, they say, "It's 10:00—do you know what time it is?"

Why don't Puerto Ricans like blow jobs?
They're afraid they'll interfere with their un-employment benefits.

What's the difference between an Italian mother and a Jewish mother?

 The Italian mother says, "If you don't eat all the food on this plate, I'll kill you."

 The Jewish mother says, "If you don't eat all the food on this plate, I'll kill myself."

What's brown and has holes in it?

 Swiss shit.

What do they use in a Mexican baptism?

 Bean dip.

Why do Mexicans eat refried beans?

 Ever seen a Mexican that didn't fuck things up the first time around?

Why is Italy shaped like a boot?

 Because they couldn't fit all that shit into a sneaker.

How does God make Puerto Ricans?

 By sandblasting blacks.

Did you hear about the Italian who picked his nose apart to see what made it run?

What's Jewish foreplay?
>A trip to the jewelry store followed by a half hour of begging.

Puerto Rican foreplay?
>"Is your husband back from work yet, Carmen?"

Black foreplay?
>"Don't scream or I'll kill you."

Did you hear about the Greek boy who left home because he didn't like the way he was being reared?
>He came back because he couldn't leave his brothers behind.

Why do Mexican women wear long skirts?
>To hide the no-pest strips.

Why do Italians bury their dead with their asses sticking up out of the ground?
>So they'll have somewhere to park their bicycles.

Know what Greek lipstick is?
>Preparation H.

What's the definition of a cad?
　　An Italian who doesn't tell his wife he's sterile until she's pregnant.

How come the Mexican Army only used 600 soldiers at the Alamo?
　　They only had two cars.

How do you kill an Italian?
　　Smash the toilet seat down on his head while he's getting a drink.

Why do Mexicans' cars have such small steering wheels?
　　So they can drive with handcuffs on.

What's the definition of a maniac?
　　An Italian in a whorehouse with a credit card.

How do you get two Mexicans off your roof?
　　Jerk one off and the other'll come too.

Who won the race down the tunnel—the black or the Pole?

The Pole, because the black had to stop and write "motherfucker" on the wall.

How many people from New Jersey does it take to change a light bulb?

Three: one to do it, one to watch, and the third to shoot the witness.

What do you call a Vietnamese family with one dog?

Vegetarians.

What do you call a Vietnamese family with two dogs?

Ranchers.

How many Mexicans does it take to grease a car?

One, if you hit 'em right.

Black

Remember how to keep little black kids from jumping up and down on the bed? (Put Velcro on the ceiling.)
How do you get 'em down?
> Invite some Mexican kids over and tell them it's a piñata party.

What's the definition of worthless?
> A seven-foot-two-inch black with a small cock who can't play basketball.

Did you hear the Harlem High school cheer?
> Barbecue, watermelon,
>> Cadillac car;
> We're not as dumb
>> As you think we is!

There was this football coach who wasn't too pleased with the way his team was performing; their record was 0–6 and it was already half way through the season. He didn't know quite what to do about it, though, since he couldn't figure out whether the play book was too complicated or whether the players were simply unable to play any better. Finally he decided that the best solution was to simplify the play book, reducing the number of plays to something even the most thick-headed guy on the team could understand.

So after a particularly depressing defeat, he called his muddy and battered team together and explained that from now on they would only have to master four plays, and that he had simplified the calls as follows: NRR, NRL, SPDN, and WBK.

"What's dat agin, coach?" asked the quarterback, scratching his head.

"NRR," explained the coach, "stands for Nigger Run Right."

"NRL," he went on, "means Nigger Run Left, and SPDN means Same Play, Different Nigger. As for WBK, well that's White Boy Kick."

What's tattooed on the inside of every negro's lip?
  Inflate to 50 psi.

Why do blacks wear high-heeled shoes?
  So their knuckles don't scrape the ground.

Why do blacks wear wide-brimmed hats?
  So pigeons don't shit on their lips.

Two black garbagemen in Atlanta were going about their rounds and came to the end of their route with the garbage truck absolutely full—and with one bag of garbage still sitting on the sidewalk. Being conscientious workers, they were reluctant to leave it, but the truck would not hold another ounce.

"Tell you what, Joe," said Sam. "You drive real slowly, and I'll hang on to the back of the truck holding that last bag with my body. We ain't got too far to go."

That was fine with Joe, and so he drove the truck off with Sam clinging, spread-eagled, to the back of the truck.

They rounded the corner and passed by two Southern gentlemen, who looked at the back end of the truck with considerable surprise. "Can you believe your eyes?" asked his companion. "They're throwing away a perfectly good nigger!"

What do you call a black millionaire physicist?
A nigger.

What do you get when you cross a black and a groundhog?
Six more weeks of basketball season.

How do you know Adam and Eve weren't black?
Ever tried to take a rib from a black man?

There was a black couple that already had eight fine children, and finally the wife implored her husband to have a vasectomy. After much cajoling, he made an appointment, and the morning of the operation his wife was astonished to see him leave the house dressed in white tie and tails and head for a big black limousine waiting at the curb. Responding to her quizzical look, he explained, "Honey, if you gonna *be* impo'tant, you gotta *act* impo'tant!"

A con man came into a small-town saloon, sidled up to the bar, and told the bartender he'd bet him $50 he could have him in tears in three minutes. "You got a deal!" said the bartender. "I haven't cried since I broke my ankle when I was ten."

So two and a half minutes went by in silence, and finally the bartender said, "You know, you only have thirty seconds left and I'm nowhere near tears."

"No problem," said the con man. "My friend Boo will be along any moment, and he'll have you bawling in no time."

"Boo who?" asked the bartender . . . and then sheepishly handed over the fifty bucks.

The con man proceeded down the bar to where a black guy was nursing a beer, and made him the same offer. "Man, ah ain' cried since ah was a baby," said the black guy. "You on!"

A minute, two minutes ticked by, and the black guy spoke up, pointing out that time was running short. "Don't you worry," said the con man, "my friend Boo is due right about now and you're going to weep."

"Who be Boo?" asked the black guy.

Did you hear about the little black kid who got diarrhea?

He thought he was melting.

What do they call a woman in the Army?
A WAC.
What do they call a black woman in the Army?
A WACcoon.

Why do blacks always have sex on their minds?
Because of the pubic hair on their heads.

A crowd gathered on a Harlem sidewalk where a white guy was jumping up and down on a manhole cover energetically, shouting, "Twenty-eight! Twenty-eight!" Finally one big black guy was unable to restrain his curiosity. "What you doin' dat fo'?" he roughly questioned the jumper.

"Listen, it really makes you feel great. You wouldn't believe how it relieves tension, cools you out... Why don't you try it for yourself?"

So, somewhat suspiciously, the big black guy started jumping up and down on the manhole cover. Just as he was getting into a rhythm, the white guy pulled the cover out from underneath him, and the black tumbled down the hole.

Cheerfully replacing the cover, the guy started jumping up and down again, shouting, "Twenty-nine! Twenty-nine!"

Did you hear about the African sex researcher?
    Kunte Kinsey.

Did you hear about the new black French restaurant?
    Chez What?

What do you call four blacks in a '57 Chevy?
    A blood vessel.

What are three French words all blacks know?
    Coupe de ville.

What's black and shines in the dark?
    Oakland.

Why did God create the orgasm?
    So blacks would know when to stop screwing.

18

What did Lincoln say after his five-day drunk?

"I freed *who*?"

Why do blacks wear white gloves?

So they don't bite off the ends of their fingers when they're eating Tootsie Rolls.

It was the first day of the new term at Princeton, and a black freshman was learning his way around the campus. Stopping a distinguished-looking upperclassman, he inquired, "Say, can you tell me where the library is at?"

"My good fellow," came the reply, "at Princeton we do not end our sentences with a preposition."

"All right," said the freshman, "can you tell me where the library is at, asshole?"

Three people die at the same moment and arrive at the gates of heaven at the same time. St. Peter greets them warmly and asks the first, "And what did you die of, may I ask?"

"The Big H," says the fellow, a florid, overweight type.

"Ah yes," nods St. Peter, "the number one killer of men your age. Please step this way."

The second person, a withered old man, attributes his death to "the Big C."

"So sorry to hear it," murmurs St. Peter. "This way, please." And to the next person in line he asks, "Cause of death?"

The big black woman says, "De big G."

"What in heavens name is 'the Big G'?"

"Dat's gonorrhea," she answers.

"Madam," says St. Peter stiffly, "one does not die of gonorrhea."

"You does if you gives it to Big Leroy."

Jewish

If Tarzan and Jane were Jewish, what would Cheetah be?

A fur coat.

What do you get when you cross a JAP and an Apple?

A computer that never goes down.

The Jewish grandmother was terribly proud of her four-month-old grandson, so she took him with her down to Miami Beach. The first morning she got him all decked out, and down they went to the beach, where she set him by the shore to play. But no sooner had she sat down in her beach chair than a huge tidal wave rose up and swept the baby away.

"God," she said, standing up and shaking her fist at the sky, "you aren't very nice! Here was this little baby boy, whose mother carried him for nine months, barely around for four. We haven't even had time to get to know him or give him a happy life."

In another instant the wave returned, setting the infant down unharmed on the sand. The grandmother looked him over, looked right back at the sky, and snapped, "He had a hat!"

Did you hear about the new brand of tires—Firestein?

They not only stop on a dime, they pick it up.

What's the difference between a JAP and a bowl of Jell-O?

Jell-O shakes when you eat it.

There was a seventy-year-old *mohel* (that's the person who performs ritual circumcisions for Jews, in case you didn't know) who found to his horror that his hands were beginning to shake. Needless to say, in his line of work that was a serious liability, and he dashed off to see if he could get some sort of insurance policy.

A week later the insurance agent called him up. "Listen," he said, "I've got some good news and some bad news."

"Let me have it," said the *mohel*.

"Well the good news is that I can get you a million-dollar policy, for one hundred dollars a year, no problem," said the agent.

Wiping his forehead in relief, the *mohel* asked, "So what's the bad news?"

"There's a two-inch deductible."

What's a JAP's favorite position?
    Facing Bloomingdale's.

What's the difference between a JAP and the Bermuda Triangle?
    The Bermuda Triangle swallows semen.

How do you know when a JAP's having an orgasm?
    She drops her emery board.

Why do JAPs only sleep with circumcised men?
    They want 20% off *everything*.

Did you hear about the new movie called *Altered Suits*?
    It's the story of a Jewish man who takes acid and buys retail.

What's the worst thing for a JAP about having a colostomy?
    Trying to find shoes to match the bag.

What did one mink say to the other as they were taken out of their cages to be killed and skinned?

"See you in Temple."

You can imagine the excitement when a Martian spaceship landed in a sunny suburban field and proved to be filled with intelligent, amicable beings. Jane Pauley managed to be the first television personality on the scene, and the chief Martian agreed to an exclusive interview on the "Today" show the next morning. As the cameras started to roll, she told the Martian how curious people on Earth were about his people, so she thought she'd just ask him a few general questions. The Martian graciously said that was fine with him.

"Tell me," said Pauley, nervously clearing her throat, "do all of your people have seven fingers and toes?"

"Yes," said the Martian, waving his slender green appendages in the air.

"And two heads? Everyone has those?"

"Oh yes," said the Martian, nodding both enthusiastically.

"And also those lovely diamonds and rubies embedded in their chests as you do?" asked Pauley.

"Certainly not," snapped the Martian. "Only the Jews."

What's the difference between a Jewish mother and a vulture?

A vulture waits till you're dead to eat your heart out.

What's a JAP's idea of natural childbirth?
　　Absolutely no makeup.

Three nice Jewish widows decided to take an exotic vacation together, so off they went to darkest Africa on a photographic safari. The expedition pitched their tents deep in the jungle and the next morning set out on their first excursion, but Naomi was too tired to go along, despite her companions' dismay. And no sooner were they out of earshot than a huge gorilla swept down from a tree, grabbed Naomi, and dragged her off to his nest to screw her mercilessly for three days. On that night, Sophie and Zelda, hysterical with grief, found a battered and bloody Naomi, semiconscious, outside their tent. Naomi was immediately airlifted back to Mount Sinai Hospital in New York where her two friends hovered by her side until, after many days, she was able to speak.

"Naomi, darling, speak to us," beseeched her friends. "Did that creature abuse you? Are you in pain? What's wrong? Say something!"

"What should I say? He never calls," sobbed Naomi, "he never writes..."

What's the difference between circumcision and crucifixion?

In a crucifixion, they throw out the whole Jew.

The devout Jew was beside himself because his son had been dating a *shiksa*, so he went to visit his rabbi. The rabbi listened solemnly to his problem, took his hand, and said, "Pray to God."

So the Jew went to the synagogue, bowed his head, and prayed, "God, please help me. My son, my favorite son, he's going to marry a *shiksa*, he sees nothing but goyim..."

"Your son," boomed down this voice from the heavens, "you think *you* got problems. What about *my* son?"

What's a JAP's dream house?

Fourteen rooms in Scarsdale, no kitchen, no bedroom.

God's cleaning house, and he comes across these Commandments taking up valuable closet space. So he goes down to earth and offers them to the Roman emperors. "Not interested; we're too busy having orgies," is the response. Next God tries the Pharaohs, but the answer comes back, "Sorry, too busy building pyramids." Finally giving up, God takes a walk in the desert, where who should He run across but Moses. "Would you be interested in some nice Commandments by any chance?" God asks.

"How much?" asks Moses.

"Why, they're free."

"I'll take ten."

Why do JAPs have crow's-feet?

From squinting and saying, "Suck *what*?"

Why do JAPs close their eyes while they're fucking?

So they can pretend they're shopping.

What's the difference between a JAP and a canoe?

Canoes tip.

What did Mr. Mink give Mrs. Mink for Christmas?

A full-length Jew.

It's quiz time in the parochial school, and Brother Michael offers a fifty cent prize to the student who can name the greatest man who ever lived.

"Columbus," offers Joey Rizzo.

"Pope John Paul II," volunteers Jan Milowski.

"St. Francis of Assisi," says Irving Feldman, whispering to a classmate, "I would've said Moses, but business is business."

27

What's a JAP's favorite wine? (Say it aloud and it sounds like "whine.")

"I wanna go to Floooorida..."

What's the difference between a JAP and a barracuda?

Nail polish.

What does a JAP do during a nuclear holocaust?

Gets out her sun reflector.

Polish

Did you hear about the Pole who heard on the radio that 90 percent of all accidents happen within a 10-mile radius of the home?

He moved.

How about the Polish abortion clinic?

There's a year-long waiting list.

One night the Pope is saying his bedtime prayers when God Himself comes down from heaven to listen to them. Then, sitting on the Pope's bed, He says, "Listen, you've been such a good Pope and devoted follower that I'm going to grant you any wish you'd like."

The Pope is overcome with emotion, and for a little while he can't think of anything to say, but then he confesses to one thing that really gets to him. "As you know, God," he says, "I'm very attached to my country of origin. And one thing that really irritates me sometimes is all those stupid Polish jokes."

"No problem," says God magnanimously. "From this moment on, there shall be no more Polish jokes." Smiling, He says, "Listen, I have to be getting back to heaven, but before I take off, is there anything else I can do?"

The Pope thinks and thinks, finally coming out with it. "M&M's," he pronounces.

"M&M's?" says God. "Gee, I've always thought they were harmless enough, melting in your mouth and all that...but I'll be glad to abolish them if it really means a lot to you."

"Well you see," says the Pope, "I'm not getting any younger, and it's getting harder and harder to peel them."

Did you hear how the Polish hockey team drowned?

Spring training.

Know how you can tell when a firing squad is Polish?

It stands in a circle.

How do you break a Pole's finger?

Hit him in the nose.

Hear about the lazy Pole?

He married a pregnant woman.

What's the smallest room in the world?
    The Polish Hall of Fame.

Hear about the Pole who went out and bought four new snow tires?
    They melted on the way home.

Or the Pole who lost $50 on the football game?
    $25 on the game and $25 on the instant replay.

Then there was the Pole who had the asshole transplant.
    The asshole rejected him.

    How about the Polish girl who wanted to trade her menstrual cycle for a Honda?

    These two Poles go for a drive in the country, and when nature calls, they stop at an outhouse in a field. One fellow goes in first, and when ten minutes go by and he's still in there, his friend walks over and says, "Stan, are you all right?" Opening the door, he sees Stan poking around in the hole with a big stick. Stan explains that he managed to drop his overcoat down the hole.

"Listen," says his friend, "forget about the coat, okay?"

"Yeah, sure," says Stan. "It's not the coat I want, it's the sandwich in the pocket."

Then there was the Polish girl who said she'd do anything for a fur coat, and now she can't button it over her belly.

Why do Polish stadiums have Astroturf?
To keep the cheerleaders from grazing.

This Polish guy ordered a pizza with everything on it. When it came out of the oven, the guy asked him if he'd like it cut into four or eight pieces. "Make it four," said the Pole. "I'll never be able to eat eight."

What's green and flies over Poland?
Peter Panski.

Did you hear about the Pole who had body odor on one side only?
He didn't know where to buy Left Guard.

What about the Polish woman who thought Moby Dick was a venereal disease?

Two Poles walk into the post office and the first thing that catches their eye is a bunch of "Wanted" posters, in particular a shot of a mean-looking black guy beneath a banner that says "Wanted for Rape."

"You know," said one Pole to his friend, "they get all the good jobs."

A Pole has a big date, so he goes to the drugstore to buy some condoms. "That'll be $2.59 plus tax," says the clerk.

"What?" exclaims the Pole. "They don't stay up by themselves?"

Two Polish girls were walking down the street on a Saturday afternoon. One looks over and notices that her friend is walking a bit oddly, with her legs far apart. "Zelda," she asks, "why are you walking like that? Is something wrong?"

"Hey, I got a big date tonight," says Zelda. "My hair's in curlers."

Why are there no ice cubes in Poland?
 They lost the recipe.

Did you hear about the Pole who keeps a store of empty beer bottles handy... for his friends who don't drink.

What do Poles say before picking their noses?
    Grace.

Joe Kowalski emigrates from Poland to America, filled with excitement at the promise his new land holds. He gets into a taxi at the airport and instructs the driver to take him to the Yimca Hotel. Perplexed, the cabbie goes over to another driver, who explains that his passenger means the YMCA. "He must be Polish—that's where they always want to go."

Joe is astonished when the cabbie asks him if he's Polish. How did he know? he wonders. He makes a vow to learn perfect English and become expert in the ways of his new country so that never again will he be taken for a foreigner, let alone a Pole. So he studies and studies, and finally decides it's time to give his English a field test. Repeating the phrase over and over to get it letter-perfect, he goes out to the corner store. Standing at the counter, he says in perfect English, "May I please have a quart of milk, a dozen eggs, and a quarter pound of Swiss cheese?"

"You Polish or something?" asks the proprietor.

"Why, yes, but... how did you know?" stammers Joe. "Did I not say it right?"

34

"You said it fine," says the fellow behind the counter, "but this is a hardware store."

Why don't Polish women breast-feed their babies?
 It hurts too much when they boil the nipples.

Why do Polish men make lousy lovers?
 Because they always wait for the swelling to go down.

What's this? (Puff out your cheeks.)
 A Polish sperm bank.

What do you call a Pole with 1500 girl friends?
 A shepherd.

Why are there no Polish ballerinas?
 Because when they do splits, they stick to the floor.

Why are "Polish" and "polish" spelled the same way?
 Because Webster didn't know shit from Shinola.

What happens when a Pole doesn't pay his garbage bill?

They don't deliver anymore.

Did you hear about the Pole who won a gold medal in the Olympic Games?

He had it bronzed.

There's this farmer with a two-seater outhouse, and one morning he happens to be sharing it with a Pole. "Dammit!" says the farmer, pulling his pants up. "I dropped a quarter in there."

"Don't worry, I'll get it for you," offers the Pole, who gets up and proceeds to pull out a five-dollar bill and throw it down the farmer's hole.

"What did you do that for?" asks the bewildered farmer.

"Hell," says the Pole, "you didn't think I'd go down there just for a quarter, did you?"

Did you hear about the Polish parachute?

It opens on impact.

This Pole got married, but he was too dumb to know what to do on his wedding night.

"For God's sake, Stan," said his bride, "you take

that thing you play with and you put it where I pee."

So he got up and threw his bowling ball in the sink.

WASP

What does a WASP do when his car breaks down?

Fixes it.

How many WASPs does it take to change a light bulb?

One.

Two WASPs were walking down the street. One turned to the other and said, "You know, you're my best friend but you never ask how I'm doing, how things are going, how's business?"

"Okay," said his friend, "how's business?"

"Fine."

What do WASPs do instead of making love?

Rule the country.

What does a WASP mom make for dinner?
   A crisp salad, a hearty soup, a lovely entree,
and a delicious dessert.

Handicapped

What do you call a guy with no arms or legs
in the swimming pool?
    Bob.

What do you call the same guy in the ocean?
    Skip.

What do you call the same guy at your door?
    Matt.

What do you call the same guy tacked up on your
wall?
    Art.

How did Helen Keller discover masturbation?
    Trying to read her own lips.

Desperate about the state of her social life, a young woman resorted to the Personals Ads in the back of her local paper. In the ad she made it quite clear that what she was advertising for was an expert lover; she already had plenty of sensitive friends and meaningful relationships and what she now wanted was to get laid, to put it bluntly.

Phone calls started coming in, with each caller testifying to his sexual prowess, but none quite struck the young woman's fancy. Until one night her doorbell rang. Opening the door, she found a man with no arms or legs. "I'm terribly sorry," she stammered, "but my ad was quite explicit. I'm really looking for something of a sexual expert, and you...uh...don't have all the..."

"Listen," the man interrupted her, "I rang the doorbell, didn't I?"

What's the hardest thing about eating vegetables?
The wheelchairs.

What's the definition of endless love?
Ray Charles and Helen Keller playing tennis.

Why do farts smell?
So deaf people can appreciate them too.

How do you tell the blind guy in a nudist colony?
　　It's not hard.

There's this really shy guy who never leaves his room. Although he's desperately lonely for any sort of companionship, he's terribly self-conscious about the fact that he has a wooden eye, and even though it's not very noticeable he doesn't want to expose himself to ridicule. Finally his best friend says, "Look, if you ever want to do anything with your life you've simply got to get out and about. Come with me to the prom on Saturday."

With the greatest reluctance he agrees, and Saturday night finds him sitting on the bleachers in the high school gym while his friend dances away, until he notices a woman on the other side of the room. She's not beautiful—in fact she has a harelip—and he screws up his courage to approach her.

"Would you like to dance?" he asks.

Her face lighting up, she cries, "Would I? Would I?"

"Harelip! Harelip!" he shouts back.

What has 30,000 feet and still can't walk?
　　Jerry's kids.

This guy has a blind date, and when she comes to the door his worst fears are realized: she's a paraplegic. But he takes her out to dinner and the movies anyway, being a nice guy, and in the movie theater it doesn't take long for things to work up to the heavy-breathing stage. Still, there she is in her wheelchair, and he's pretty perplexed about how to take things to the next stage...if there's going to *be* a next stage.

"Don't worry," she whispers in his ear. "Take me to the playground, and I'll hang from the jungle gym."

So he does just that, and they manage to have a pretty good time. She gets a little dirty and scratched up in the process though, and he's somewhat apprehensive when her father comes to the door to let her in.

"You see, sir..." he begins, but her father interrupts him with effusive thanks. "Don't worry about a thing, young man. The last three guys left her hanging there."

Did you hear the one about the queer deaf mute?
    Neither did he.

What goes, "Marc! Marc!"?
    A dog with a harelip.

What goes, "Nort! Nort!"?
    A bull with a cleft palate.

More Jokes
for the Blind

Male Anatomy

This fellow married a virgin and wanted to go to special pains to make sure her sexual inexperience wasn't to be a cause of any tension or trouble. He explained that he didn't ever want her to feel pressured into having sex with him, but wanted it to come of her own free will. "In fact, darling," he said to her tenderly, "I think we should set up a little system in code to make all this as simple as possible. Here's how it'll work: when you want to have sex, pull my penis once; when you don't want to have sex, pull my penis a hundred times."

What did the Pole do before going to the cockfight?
> Greased his zipper.

What's the difference between "ooh" and "aah"?
> About three inches.

What do you get when you cross a rooster and a telephone pole?

A thirty-foot cock that wants to reach out and touch someone.

Did you hear about the man who couldn't spell?

He spent the night in a warehouse.

Why can't you circumcise Iranians?

There's no end to those pricks.

One night after their proprietor was asleep, the parts of the body were arguing about which had the toughest job. "I've really got it rough," bemoaned the feet. "He puts me in these smelly sneakers, makes me jog till I've got blisters . . . it's brutal!"

"You got nothing to complain about," maintained the stomach. "Last night I got nothing but bourbon, pizza, and aspirin. It's a miracle I kept it together."

"Oh quit bitching, you two," moaned the penis. "Every night, I'm telling you, he sticks me in a dark tunnel and makes me do push-ups until I throw up."

There once was a pro football player called Smithers, whose main role was warming the bench. Every game he would put on his pads, smear his cheeks with charcoal, don his helmet and run out onto the field with the rest of the team; but play after play, game after game, season after season went by without Smithers ever being called into action.

One Saturday near the end of the season Smithers was feeling lousy. "Helene," he asked his long-time girl friend, "I want you to do me a favor. Dress up in my uniform, smear your face, put on my helmet, and sit on the bench for me this game. You know I never play, and nobody'll ever know."

Helene required some additional convincing but finally agreed, and sure enough, no one on Smithers's team gave her the time of day. The first half passed without event; she hung out in the locker room during halftime; the third quarter went by smoothly, and it wasn't until the last quarter that one man after another started falling to injuries. The bench grew emptier and emptier and finally, in desperation, the coach barked, "Smithers, get in there!"

Rather panicked, Helene went out onto the field, crouched down in the lineup, and was knocked cold within the first three seconds of play. When she came to, the coach was vigorously massaging her pussy. "Don't worry, Smithers," he said nervously, "once we get your balls back in place, your cock'll pop right up."

What's the definition of conceit?
> A mosquito with a hard-on floating down the river on his back shouting, "Open the draw-bridge!"

An international conference of sexologists was convened to determine once and for all why the penis is shaped the way it is. Each national delegation had done extensive research and was to announce its results.

Said the French spokesman, "We have spent five million francs and can now firmly state zat ze penis is ze shape it is in order to give pleasure to ze woman."

"I say," said the British representative, "we've spent thirty thousand pounds and are quite sure that the shape is in order to give maximum pleasure to the man."

"We've spent a million bucks," drawled the American, "and there's no further doubt about the fact that it's that shape so your hand doesn't slip off the end."

What's the dumbest part of a man?

His prick. (It's got no brains, its best friends are two nuts, and it lives next door to an asshole.)

When Paddy O'Brian died, Father Flannigan was there to console the bereaved widow. "You know, Molly, the whole community is here to help you through this time of sorrow," he said, "and of course you know I'll do anything I can for you."

Parting her veil and drying her tear-stained cheeks, the widow whispered a single request in Father Flannigan's ear. The priest blushed scarlet and refused outright, but the widow continued her pleas and finally he gave in. He left, saying, "Give me twenty-four hours."

The next day he showed up at the house with something in a brown paper bag.

The widow popped the contents into a pot on the stove, and it was boiling away when a neighbor dropped by. "I say, Molly," said the neighbor opening the lid, "isn't that Paddy's penis?"

"Indeed it is," said Molly. "All his life I had to eat it his way, and now I'm eating it mine."

What three two-letter words can best dampen a man's ardor in bed?

"Is it in?"

How can a real man tell when his girl friend's having an orgasm?

Real men don't care.

What's a guy with a 12-inch cock have for breakfast?

Well, this morning I had two eggs over easy, whole wheat toast, and coffee...

What has a thousand teeth and eats wienies?

A zipper.

What do you get when you cross a penis and a potato?

A dicktater.

Did you hear about the guy who got his vasectomy done at Sears?

Every time he gets a hard-on, the garage door goes up.

A woman sought the advice of a sex therapist, confiding that she found it increasingly difficult to find a man who could satisfy her, and that it was very wearisome getting in and out of all these short-term relationships. "Isn't there some way to judge the size of a man's equipment from the outside?" she asked earnestly.

"The only foolproof way," counseled the therapist, "is by the size of his feet."

So the woman went downtown and proceeded to cruise the streets, until she came across a young fellow standing in an unemployment line with the biggest feet she had ever laid eyes on. She took him out to dinner, wined and dined him, and then took him back to her apartment for an evening of abandon.

When the man woke up the next morning, the woman had already gone out. By the bedside table was a $20 bill and a note that read, "With my compliments, take this money and go out and buy a pair of shoes that fit you."

What's the difference between anxiety and panic?
Anxiety is the first time you can't do it a second time, and panic is the second time you can't do it the first time.

This 600-pound guy decides he can't go on living this way, so he seeks the help of a clinic and proceeds to go on a drastic diet. It works: four months later he's down to 160 pounds and feeling great, except for one problem. He's covered with great folds of flesh where the fat used to be.

He calls up the clinic, and the doctor tells him not to worry. "There's a special surgical procedure to correct this condition," the doctor assures him. "Just come on over to the clinic."

"But doctor," says the one-time fatty, "you don't understand. I'm too embarrassed to be seen in public like this."

"Don't give it another thought," says the doctor. "Simply pull up all the folds as high as they'll go, pile the flesh on top of your head, put on a top hat, and come on over."

The guy follows the instructions and provokes no comments until he reaches the clinic and is standing in front of the admitting nurse's desk, dying of self-consciousness.

"The doctor will be right with you," says the nurse. "Say, what's that hole in the middle of your forehead?"

"My belly button," blurts out the guy, "how d'ya like my tie?"

Did you hear about the flasher who decided to retire?

Yeah, but he changed his mind and decided to stick it out another year.

Female Anatomy

What do you call a woman who can suck a golf ball through fifty feet of garden hose?
Darling.

What's the perfect woman?
A deaf, dumb, and blind nymphomaniac who owns a liquor store.

This well-to-do suburban matron makes an appointment for her annual checkup with a new gynecologist. Following the examination, he ushers her into his office to give her the results. "You'll be glad to hear that everything is absolutely in order," he says, leaning forward with a smile. "In fact, you have the cleanest vagina I've ever seen."

"It should be," she snaps. "I've got a colored man coming in twice a week."

A young lady went out on a date with a young man she found quite attractive, so after dinner and the movies she invited him back to her apartment. Sitting him down on her couch with a drink, she proceeded to nibble on his ear, play with his hair, and so on, but the fellow only pulled up his collar and rubbed his hands together for warmth. The young lady pulled out all the stops, sitting on his lap, even directing his hands to appropriate portions of her anatomy. But he took no action whatsoever and violently resisted her efforts to unbutton even a single one of his outer garments.

Finally in desperation, after a particularly passionate kiss had met with no response, she said, "You know, I have a hole down here."

"Oh," he said with evident relief, "so that's where the draft is coming from!"

It was late at night, and the tired cabbie was on his last run of the night. Reaching the destination, he said to the little old lady in the back seat, "That'll be eight bucks, please."

There was no answer, so thinking her hearing might be at fault, he said loudly, "Lady, the fare is eight bucks."

Still no response. So he turned around, only to be greeted by the sight of the elderly woman hoisting her skirts and spreading her legs, no underwear impairing his view.

"Well, sonny," she cackled, "will this be payment enough?"

"Aw, lady," he sighed, "doncha have anything smaller?"

What do you call a JAP's nipple?

    The tip of the iceberg.

Why do women like hunters?

    Three reasons:

    They go deep into the bush.

    They always shoot twice.

    And they always eat what they shoot.

This middle-aged woman decides she's not getting any younger and that it's time to spice up her sex life. Since she has always had a crush on the Beatles, she goes to the local tattooist with a very specific request. "I would like John Lennon tattooed on the inside of my right thigh, looking up," she instructs him, "and Paul McCartney on the left thigh, looking up. Now, are you sure you can handle this?"

The tattooist assures her that he's the best in the business, and sets to work.

A week or two later, the recuperation period is over. The woman takes off the bandages and goes over to her mirror in great anticipation, only to discover that to her horror the two portraits bear no resemblance at all to Lennon and McCartney. She rushes over to the tattooist's office in a rage.

"I don't see what you're complaining about," he says soothingly. "I think the likenesses are astonishing. But clearly we need a third, unbiased opinion." So he goes out to the sidewalk and brings back the first person he encounters, a wino still reeling from the night before. Confronting him with the evidence, the tattooist asks the wino, "Now on that right side, does that look like John Lennon?"

"I dunno," says the wino after a long silence.

"Well, how about the left one?" asks the tattooist. "Is that or is that not the spitting image of Paul McCartney?"

"I dunno," says the wino after considerable thought. "But that guy in the middle with the beard and the bad breath, that's *gotta* be Willie Nelson."

What's the only thing used sanitary napkins are good for?

Tea bags for vampires.

Why does it take women longer to climax?

Who cares?

How can you tell if a Polish woman is having her period?

She's only wearing one sock.

What's the latest disease in Poland?

Toxic Sock Syndrome!

Three guys were sitting around in a bar discussing whose wife was the most frigid. Harry was definitely sure he had the worst of it. "Listen, you guys," he said, "my wife comes to bed with an ice cube in each hand, and in the morning they haven't begun to melt."

"That's *nothing*," said Phil. "My wife likes to have a glass of water on the bedside table, but by the time she's carried it from the bathroom to the bedroom, it's frozen solid."

"Aw, hell," said Herb, "my wife is so frigid that when she spreads her legs, the furnace kicks on."

What's the difference between a magician and a chorus line?

A magician has cunning feats and stunts.

God has just spent six days creating the heavens and the earth, and since it's the seventh day of rest, He and Gabriel are sitting back and admiring His handiwork.

"You know, God," says Gabriel, "you have done one hell of a job—excuse my language. Those snowy peaks are unbelievably majestic, and the woods, with those little sunny dells and meadows...masterful. Not to mention the oceans: those fantastic coral reefs and all the sea creatures and the waves crashing on the beaches. And all the animals—from fleas to elephants—what a job. Not to mention the heavens; how could I leave them out? What a touch, that Milky Way."

God beams.

"I just have the smallest suggestion, if you'll excuse my presumption," says Gabriel. "You know those sample humans you put down there in the Garden of Eden?"

God nods, a frown furrowing His brow.

"Well," says Gabriel, "I was just wondering whether, for all the obvious reasons, they shouldn't have differing sets of genitalia as all the other animals do?"

God reflects on this for a minute, and then a smile crosses His face. "You're right," He exclaims. "Give the dumb one a cunt!"

When you order a Bloody Mary, how can you tell if the waitress is mad at you?

She leaves the string in.

Why do women rub their eyes when they get out of bed in the morning?

Because they don't have balls to scratch.

Mrs. Smith was quite embarrassed when little Johnny burst into the shower, pointed at her pubic hair, and asked loudly, "What's that, Mommy?"

"That's my sponge, honey," she explained.

She was even more embarrassed when Johnny burst in a week later, because, to satisfy one of Mr. Smith's kinkier requests, she had shaved herself. In answer to Johnny's question, she hastily explained that she had lost her sponge. "It got dirty, honey, and I threw it out the window."

Johnny was gone for a couple of hours, but came back with a big grin on his face. "I found your sponge, Mommy," he cried. "I looked in the Browns' window, and Mrs. Brown was washing Mr. Brown's face with it!"

There was great excitement in the laboratory when the eminent scientist announced a new invention—the apple. That was nothing new, his colleagues pointed out; the apple had been around for a long time.

"Yes, but this apple tastes like pussy," proudly explained the scientist. "Try it."

A skeptical fellow took a big bite, only to spit it out all over the floor. "It tastes like *shit*," he said disgustedly.

"Indeed," said the scientist. "Turn it around."

What's the function of a woman?
    Life-support system for a pussy.

What do you call a truckload of vibrators?
    Toys for twats.

The elementary school lesson for the day was The Farm. "All right, children," said the teacher, "who can tell me the name of the big building all the animals sleep in?"

"The barn," piped up Melissa.

"Very good, Melissa. And who knows the name of the tall, cylindrical building next to the barn that the farmer stores the grain in?"

"The silo," said Susie.

"Right, Susie. And who knows what the little metal bird up on the roof of the barn is called, class? Mark?"

"That's...uh...the weather-thing."

"Well, you're right, Mark, it is for telling us something about the weather. But who can tell us what the exact name is, and why?"

"It's a weathercock," explained Davey, "because if it were a weathercunt the wind would blow right through it."

How can you tell if a woman is wearing panty-hose?

If her ankles swell up when she farts.

Why are hockey goaltenders and Polish girls alike?

They both change their pads after three periods.

Did you hear about the Italian girl who thought a sanitary belt was a drink from a clean shot glass?

Cinderella is thrilled about her invitation to the ball, but her feelings soon turn to dismay when she realizes she has nothing but rags to wear. "Don't worry," says her fairy godmother, and—*Poof*—a beautiful gown and sparkling pair of slippers instantly appear. "But there's a condition," warns the godmother as Cinderella preens in front of the mirror. "You must be home by midnight or your pussy will turn into a pumpkin."

The dazzling Cinderella soon captures the heart of the most handsome man at the ball, and they are dancing away rapturously—until Cinderella remembers to look at her watch. "Oh my God," she gasps. "It's almost midnight! I must be going." But the young man runs after her as she makes for the door, begging her to stay and insisting that she at least give him her name so that he can find her again.

"My name is Cinderella," she says. "What's yours?"

"Peter Peter Pumpkin Eater," says he.

"Oh, in *that* case I'll stay."

Harry was delighted when he found a young woman who accepted his proposal of marriage, as he was sensitive about his wooden leg and a bit afraid no one would have him. In fact, he couldn't bring himself to tell his fiancée about his leg when he slipped the ring on her finger, nor when she bought the dress, nor when they picked the time and place. All he kept saying was, "Darling, I've got a big surprise for you," at which she blushed and smiled bewitchingly.

The wedding itself came and went, and the young couple were at last alone in their hotel room. "Now don't forget, Harry, you promised me a big surprise," said the bride.

Unable to say a word, Harry turned out the lights, unstrapped his wooden leg, slipped into bed, and placed his wife's hand on the stump.

"Hmmmmm," she said softly, "that *is* a surprise. But pass me the Vaseline, and I'll see what I can do."

Fred's wife refused to wear underwear, and it drove him crazy. He didn't think it was proper or sanitary or right, but nothing he said persuaded her to mend her ways. But when she caught a bad cold one winter, Fred had a brainstorm. Calling up the family doctor, he said, "Doc, I wish you'd come and look in on my wife; she's got a terrible cold. And there's something else you could do for me. You see, she's got this terrible habit of going around without any underwear on, and if you could somehow persuade her that the cold was linked to that, why, I'd pay you double."

The doctor came right over and found the woman wrapped in a blanket on the living room sofa, blowing her nose. Looking down her throat, the doctor said, "Mrs. Brown, I'll give you something for this cold . . . but if you don't start wearing underpants, it's going to bother you all winter."

"You mean to tell me, doctor," she said, "that you can tell from looking down my throat that I'm not wearing panties?"

"That's right," he assured her.

"Well then, would you mind looking up my asshole and letting me know if my hat's on straight?"

This couple is lying in bed one morning, and she takes it in mind to tell him the dream she had the night before. "Honey, I dreamed I was at a cock auction: there were extra-large cocks going for $90 or so, medium-size cocks selling for $50, and itty-bitty ones for $1.50."

"Say, was mine in the auction?" the man inquires a bit anxiously.

"Honey, yours would've been too big to get in the door."

A couple of days later they're lying in bed again, and the man says, "You wouldn't believe what I dreamed last night: that I was at a pussy auction. There were great big ones, and little hairy ones, oh, all kinds."

"Well, did you see mine?" she asks.

"Baby," he says, "the auction was *in* your pussy."

The divorce case was an especially acrimonious one, as the wife was suing on the grounds that her husband had completely failed to satisfy her. "Frankly," she advised the court in a stage whisper, "he was so poorly endowed—and I mean tiny—that it just wasn't even worth the effort."

The sympathetic judge awarded a large cash settlement to the woman, and as she left the stand

and walked past her husband, she hissed, "So long, sucker."

Sticking a finger in each corner of his mouth and pulling it as wide as possible, he said, "So long, bitch."

What do soybeans and dildos have in common?
    They're both meat substitutes.

What do eating pussy and the Mafia have in common?
    One slip of the tongue and you're in deep shit.

What's worse than getting raped by Jack the Ripper?
    Getting fingered by Captain Hook.

Why is it so groovy to be a test-tube baby?
    Because you've got a womb with a view.

Mel and Howie are frequent fishing partners, but Howie always catches more fish than Mel. One Saturday morning they're out on the lake, and Howie's pulled in a couple of nice-sized bass. Mel notices Howie sniffing his bait before putting it on the hook.

"How come?" he asks his friend.

"I have this friend who works in an autopsy room," explains Howie, "and he slips me the cunts. They make great bait."

"I can see that," says Mel. "But why do you smell them?"

"Every so often he slips in an asshole."

Why did a fellow trade in his wife for an outhouse? The hole was smaller and the smell was better.

There was this girl who lived in New Jersey, and she loved it so much that she named parts of her body after places in the Garden State. One night she confided this to her boyfriend as he was beginning to feel up her right tit. "I bet you call this Mount Pleasant," he said, and she smiled in assent.

Working his hand down her ass, he asked, "And this?"

"I call that Freehole," said she.

Getting hot and heavy, he maneuvered his hand around to the front. "I bet you call this Cherry Hill," he said triumphantly.

"Nope. That's Eatontown."

Why do women have two holes so close together? In case you miss.

If God hadn't meant us to eat pussy, He wouldn't have made it look like a taco.

Did you hear about the bride who was so horny she carried a bouquet of batteries?

Homosexual

There are these two gay guys who decide they want to have a baby. So they find an obliging lesbian, have her impregnated by sperm donation, and are simply thrilled when she gives birth to a seven-pound baby boy. They rush to the hospital for the first viewing of their son, standing with their noses pressed against the glass of the nursery window and surveying row upon row of squalling infants. Except for one quiet, clean little baby, cooing softly to itself amid all the chaos.

Sure enough, when the gays ask to see their son, the nurse heads for the quiet baby and brings him over for the proud parents to ogle.

"Gee," said one of them to the nurse, "he sure is well behaved compared to the rest of those howling brats, isn't he?"

"Oh, he's quiet now," said the nurse, "but he squalls like all the rest when I take the pacifier out of his ass."

Two gay guys, Larry and Phil, were driving down the highway when they were rear-ended by a huge semi. Somewhat shaken, they maneuvered over to the side of the road, where Phil instructed Larry to get out and confront the truck driver. "Tell him we're going to sue, sue, sue!" he shrieked.

Obligingly Larry got out and went around to the cab of the truck to deliver this message to the huge, burly driver, whose response was to snarl, "Ah, why doncha suck my cock."

"Phil," said Larry coming back to their car, "I think we're going to be able to settle out of court."

What do you call a lesbian Eskimo?
    A Klondike.

How do you identify a bull dyke?
    She kick-starts her vibrator and rolls her own tampons.

What do you get when you cross a gay Eskimo and a black?
    A snowblower that doesn't work.

This guy is taking a leak in a public men's room when a man enters with his arms held out from his sides, bent at the elbows with his hands dangling awkwardly, and comes over to him. "Would you do me a favor and unzip my fly?" he asks.

Figuring the man to be a poor cripple, perhaps an accident victim, the guy obliges, not without a flush of embarrassment when the man next requests that he take out his prick and hold it in the appropriate position.

"Shake it off" is the next instruction, then "zip me up," and the guy follows orders, wincing at his own embarrassment and at the shame of being so helpless.

"Say, thanks," says the man, flouncing to the door. "I guess my nails are dry now."

What's the definition of confusion?
    Twenty blind lesbians in a fish market.

What's the definition of a Bloody Mary?
    A wounded faggot.

What do you call a lesbian opera singer?
    A muff diva.

How can you tell when your roommate's gay?
    When his cock tastes like shit.

Did you hear about the gay Catholic?
    He couldn't decide whether the Pope was fabulous or simply divine.

Is it better to be born black or gay?
>Black, because you don't have to tell your parents.

What's this? (Stick out your tongue.)
>A lesbian with a hard-on.

How can you tell if you walk into a gay church?
>Only half the congregation is kneeling.

Did you hear about the queer Indian?
>He jumped into a canoe, took three strokes, and shot across the lake.

How about the queer burglar?
>He couldn't blow the safe, so he went down on the elevator.

What do lesbians like better than Calvin Klein jeans?
>Billy Jeans.

Why don't senators use bookmarks?
>They just bend over the pages.

Why do gay men have mustaches?
    To hide the stretch marks.

What do you call the zipper on a gay Italian's pants?
    A Mediterranean fruit fly.

What's the definition of analingus?
    Tongue-in-cheek.

Herbie had always done well in school and was doing even better in college, so his parents were a bit surprised to be summoned by the guidance counselor.

"I have some good news and some bad news, Mr. and Mrs. Robinson," said the counselor. "The bad news is that Herbie is gay."

Herbie's parents blanched.

"The good news is that he's going to be Homecoming Queen."

Religion

Why doesn't Jesus eat M&Ms?

They keep falling through the holes in his hands.

What did Jesus say to Mary while he was on the cross?

"Can you get my flats? These spikes are *killing* me."

Why did they crucify Jesus instead of stoning him to death?

Because it's easier to cross yourself than to pound yourself all over. (Note: This joke requires the accompanying gestures.)

Late one night the Pope's most intimate council of senior advisors requests admission to His Holiness's bedchamber, bearing news of the greatest urgency. They tell him that it has just been re-

vealed by sacred divinations that unless the Pope
sleeps with a woman, the Vatican State—indeed
all of Catholicism—will come to a sudden and terrible end.

The Pope thinks it over for a few minutes, and
then agrees to go ahead with the profane deed.
"But," he says, "I have three stipulations.

"First, she must be blind, so she cannot see
where she is being taken.

"Second, she must be deaf, so she cannot speak
of what has happened to her.

"And third, she must have big tits."

Why didn't Jesus get into college?
    He got hung up on his boards.

"The question for today, boys and girls," said
Sister Mary, "is, 'What part of the body goes to
heaven first?'"

Dirty Eddie was sitting in the front row waving
his hand wildly, but since his answers were usu-
ally less than satisfactory, Sister Mary refrained
from calling on him. "Yes, Veronica?"

"The heart, Sister Mary, because that's where
God's love touches you."

"Very good," said Sister Mary. "Yes, Marilyn?"

"The soul, Sister Mary, because that's the im-
mortal part of us."

"Very good, Marilyn," said Sister Mary, ob-
serving with dismay that Dirty Eddie's hand was
still waving. "Yes, Eddie?"

"The feet, Sister, the feet."

"Well, that's a curious answer, Eddie. Why the feet?"

"Because I've seen Ma with her feet up in the air, shouting, 'I'm coming, God, I'm coming!'"

This nice guy dies and goes to heaven, where he is shown to a simple hut, dressed in a plain cotton robe, and offered wine and cheese. He had anticipated something a little fancier but all his needs are cared for, so he settles in happily... until, on his daily stroll, he comes across a fellow he had known on earth to be a scoundrel and criminal. This fellow is lounging on a luxurious cloud with a gorgeous blonde, dressed in a sumptuous toga, and is holding a bottle of Chivas Regal.

All upset, the nice guy goes to talk to St. Peter. "Listen, St. Peter, on earth I was a great guy, never hurt anyone, never cheated, never stole, and all I get in heaven is a grass hut and some cheap wine. And there's this guy who lied to his mother, stole from his brother, and tortured his sister, living in the lap of luxury. It's not fair!"

"It's not all it's cut out to be, my son," smiles St. Peter. "He's got a bottle of scotch with a hole in it and a beautiful blonde without one."

How do you know Christ wasn't born in Italy?
They couldn't find three wise men and a virgin.

A white guy and a black guy were having an argument as to whether God was white or black. So they booked a flight to the Holy Land, trekked up Mt. Sinai, and shouted their question up toward the sky as loudly as possible.

"I AM WHAT I AM," boomed down the earth-shaking response.

"You *see*," said the white guy, turning around to his friend triumphantly.

"Whaddaya mean?" asked the black guy. "What does that prove?"

"Listen, if He were black, he would have said, 'I is what I is.'"

This Irish lawyer dies and arrives at the Pearly Gates at the same time as the Pope. The Pope is assigned to a hovel and given a dry crust of bread, while the lawyer is ushered into a huge mansion where a staff of servants is placed at his disposal.

"What's the story?" the Pope angrily demands of St. Peter. "I was the head of the whole Catholic church and I'm stuck in a hovel, and you give this lawyer the run of the place..."

"Well, your Holiness," gently explained St. Peter, "we have literally hundreds of Popes here in heaven, but we've never had an Irish lawyer before."

Moses and Jesus are out fishing on the Sea of Galilee and the conversation comes around to miracles. "I'd sure like to perform one," says Moses, "but I'm a bit out of shape—it's been 4000 years since my last one." Jesus urges him on, so Moses goes up to the bow of the boat, raises both arms out above the waters, and commands them to part. With a great roar, the sea parts to reveal a seabed dry as a bone, then comes together again at Moses' second command. "Not bad, eh?" says Moses, settling back down in the stern. "Think you can match that?"

"No problem," says Jesus. "After all it's only been 2000 years since this last trick." He jumps nimbly up onto the gunwale of the boat and steps gracefully out onto the water—only to sink like a stone. Moses hauls him aboard, choking and sputtering, and Jesus insists on trying again, but with the same ignominious result.

With considerable difficulty Moses gets Jesus aboard the second time, and can barely keep from laughing at the dejected heap on the bottom of the boat. "I don't know what it could be," says Jesus sadly, "except the first time around I didn't have these holes in my feet..."

A naive young priest is moved to a parish in a bad neighborhood of Manhattan and is quite bewildered by the legion of hookers who are constantly approaching him to whisper, "Five bucks for a blow job, buddy."

Finally he can stand being in ignorance no longer, and approaches one of the nuns. "Excuse my presumption, Sister," says the young priest, "but could you please tell me what a blow job is?"

"Five bucks, just like anywhere else," she replies.

The Pope is working on a crossword puzzle one Sunday afternoon. He stops for a moment or two, scratches his forehead, then asks the Cardinal, "Can you think of a four-letter word for 'woman' that ends in 'u-n-t?'"

"Aunt," replies the Cardinal.

"Say, thanks," says the Pope. "You got an eraser?"

Mother Theresa comes to New York and is greeted by a welcoming committee, who want to know what in New York she is particularly interested in seeing. "Well, to tell the truth," she says modestly, "I have always wanted to see St. Patrick's Cathedral."

"No problem," assures the head of the committee. "Not only will you see it, we'll clear everyone out and you'll have the whole church to yourself."

At the appointed hour Mother Theresa shows up at the church, where she is ushered in by a respectful prelate and left in solitude. It's only a matter of minutes before God's voice booms down from heaven. "Mother Theresa, you have been an exemplary member of the church all your life, a model for millions. Is there anything, anything at all, that I can do for you while you're here?"

"Actually, yes, there is, God," says Mother Theresa. "I've always wanted to direct."

God gets the word up in heaven that the U.S.A. is a pretty depraved place. Not having the time to spare Himself, He sends Mother Theresa down to earth as His delegate. Her instructions are to visit each of the metropolitan centers and to report back to heaven on what she finds.

The first report isn't long in coming. New York, Mother Theresa says, is filled with unimaginable sin and violence and she is leaving immediately. Boston is no better, however, being full of child molesters, and the cities of the South are no better, with heavy drinkers and sex offenders everywhere. Mother Theresa's next stop is Chicago, but she can't stand the depravity there for more than a few days, and she hops on a plane to Los Angeles.

No word for three weeks. God finally gets concerned, and He gets her number from Information and calls her up. "Terri here," comes on a mellow voice. "I'm not home right now, but if you'd like to share your thoughts..."

New slogan: Save Soviet Jewry—Win Valuable Prizes.

Famous Dead People

What did Grace Kelly have that Natalie Wood could've used?
  A good stroke.

Did you hear the new national anthem of Monaco?
  "She'll Be Comin' 'Round the Mountain When She Comes..."

Did you hear Prince Rainier finally got some good news?
  The car is covered by insurance.

Did you know that Princess Grace was on the radio?
  And on the dashboard and on the steering wheel...

What would Princess Grace be doing if she were alive today?

Scratching at the inside of her coffin.

Did you hear about the new Vic Morrow movie?

Blade Runner II. It's being made in two parts.

One day in heaven John Lennon was sitting around looking pretty blue. Luckily Steve McQueen was on the next cloud over, and he came by and asked Lennon how come he was so down-in-the-mouth.

"Oh, I miss Yoko and Sean and my fans, I guess," said Lennon. "It's just not as much fun being dead as it was being alive."

"Well cheer up," said McQueen, "I'm having a party."

So Lennon was looking pretty cheerful when Bob Marley drifted by a few hours later. "What's happening, mon?" he asked. "Why you look so cheerful?"

"Steve McQueen's having a party and I'm invited," explained Lennon happily, only to have his face fall when Marley told him the party had been cancelled. "How come?" he asked dejectedly.

"Bobby Sands came early," explained Marley, "and he ate all the food."*

---

*Please keep in mind the gruesome deaths of all of these people. Bobby Sands was an Irish hunger striker, remember?

How did they know Vic Morrow had dandruff?
    They found his head and shoulders in the
    bushes.

Who taught Grace Kelly to drive?
    Ted Kennedy.

What kind of wood doesn't float?
    Natalie Wood.

Why doesn't Natalie shower on the boat?
    She prefers to wash up on shore.

What's blue and sings alone?
    Dan Ackroyd.

What's the difference between a moose and Guy
Lombardo's orchestra?
    With a moose, the horns are in front and the
    asshole's in the rear.

Did you hear Grace Kelly and Patricia Neal were
to have made a movie together?
    Called *Different Strokes*.

Did you know Vic Morrow's been made an honorary member of the Rotary Club?

You know what's next door to the Joan Crawford Daycare Center in Hollywood?

> The Grace Kelly Driving School. (Also the store where they sell Natalie Wood Water Wings and the William Holden Drinking Helmet.)

Animals

A young man was delighted to finally be asked home to meet the parents of the young woman he'd been seeing for some time. He was quite nervous about the meeting, though, and by the time he arrived punctually at the doorstep he was in a state of gastric distress. The problem developed into one of acute flatulence, and half-way through the canapés the young man realized he couldn't hold it in one second longer without exploding. A tiny fart escaped.

"Spot!" called out the young woman's mother to the family dog, lying at the young man's feet.

Relieved at the dog's having been blamed, the young man let another, slightly larger one go.

"Spot!" she called out sharply.

"I've got it made," thought the fellow to himself. One more and I'll feel fine. So he let loose a really big one.

"*Spot!*" shrieked the mother. "Get over here before he shits on you!"

If a stork delivers white babies and a crow delivers black babies, what kind of bird delivers no babies?

A swallow.

What do you call a dog with no legs?

    Nothing. He can't come when you call anyway.

What do you get when you cross a deer and a pickle?

    A dildo.

This little kid is taking a walk with his father around the neighborhood and what should they come across in an empty lot but two dogs going at it furiously. "Daddy," asked the kid, tugging on his father's sleeve, "what are those dogs doing?"

"Well, Billy," said his father, "they're making puppies."

A week later Billy gets thirsty in the middle of the night and wanders into his parents' bedroom, catching them in the act. "Daddy," he asks plaintively, "what are you and Mommy doing?"

"Well, Billy," says his slightly red-faced father, "we're making babies."

"Daddy, Daddy," cries Billy, "roll her over—I'd rather have puppies."

What do you call a cow who's had an abortion?

    Decaffeinated.

What do a walrus and Tupperware have in common?

They both like a tight seal.

What's the last thing that goes through a bug's mind before hitting the windshield at 80 mph?

Its asshole.

A man was surprised by the sight of a fellow walking down the sidewalk holding a three-legged pig on a leash. Unable to restrain his curiosity, he crossed the street and said to the guy, "That's quite a pig you have there."

"Let me tell you about this pig," said the guy. "This pig is the most amazing animal that ever lived. Why, one night my house caught on fire when my wife and I were out, and this pig carried my three children to safety and put out the fire before the firemen could get there."

"Wow!" said the first man. "But what about..."

"And that's not all," interrupted the guy. "My house was broken into when my wife and I were sound asleep, and this pig had the valuables back in place and the thief in a half Nelson before we got to the bottom of the stairs."

"That's pretty impressive," conceded his listener. "But how come..."

"And listen to this!" burst in the guy. "When I fell through some thin ice while skating, this pig dove in and pulled me out and safely to shore. This pig saved my life!"

"That's really great," said the first man, "but I have to know one thing. How come the pig only has three legs?"

"Hey listen," replied the proud owner, "a pig like this you can't eat all at once."

What's brown and white, lives in the forest, and doesn't have a mother?

Bambi.

This hot and dusty cowboy rode in from the mesa, filthy and exhausted. He obviously had had nothing but his horse for company for a couple of weeks and was looking forward to a couple of cold beers in the saloon. Swinging off his horse and hitching it to the rail, the cowboy gave his horse an affectionate slap on the neck. Then he astonished an old cowhand lounging on the porch by moving around to the horse's hindquarters, lifting up its tail, and planting a demure kiss on its asshole.

"What'd you do *that* for?" asked the cowhand, completely repulsed.

"Chapped lips," said the cowboy, heading for the saloon doors.

"Wait a minute," said the old guy. "Whaddaya mean, chapped lips?"

"Keeps ya from lickin' 'em," explained the cowboy.

Why don't bunnies make noise when they screw?
    They have cotton balls.

A guy returns from a long trip to Europe, having left his beloved cat in his brother's care. The minute he's cleared customs, he calls up his brother and inquires after his pet.

"Your cat's dead," replies his brother bluntly.

The guy is devastated. "You know how much that cat meant to me," he moaned into the phone. "Couldn't you at least have thought of a nicer way of breaking the news? Couldn't you have said, 'Well, you know, the cat got out of the house one day and climbed up on the roof, and the fire department couldn't get her down, and finally she died of exposure...or starvation...or something'? Why are you always so thoughtless?"

"Look, I'm sorry," said his brother. "I'll try to do better next time."

"Okay, let's just put it behind us. How are you, anyway? How's Mom?"

His brother is silent a moment. "Uh," he stammers, "uh...Mom's on the roof."

Why does Miss Piggy douche with vinegar and honey?
    Kermit likes sweet-and-sour pork.

This guy walks into a psychiatrist's office with a duck on his head. "May I help you?" politely inquires the psychiatrist.

"Yeah," says the duck. "Get this guy off my ass."

What's the difference between a rooster and a whore?

A rooster says cock-a-doodle-doo; a whore says, "Any cock'll do."

How about the difference between a rooster and a lawyer?

A rooster clucks defiance...

Do you know why the British ships came back from the Falkland Islands full of sheep?

War brides.

This big black guy comes into a bar in the deep South with an alligator on a leash. "You serve martinis?" he asks the bartender, who's eyeing him suspiciously.

"Yes, we do."

"You serve niggers?"

"Yes, we do."

"I'll have a martini for myself," says the guy, "and a nigger for my alligator."

What do elephants use for condoms?

Goodyear blimps.

Why did the rooster cross the basketball court?
He heard the ref was blowing fouls.

Why does an elephant have four feet?
Eight inches isn't enough.

Where's an elephant's sex organ?
In his feet. If he steps on you, you're fucked.

What do you do when you come across an elephant?
Wipe it off.

Did you hear about the alligators in Florida sporting little Jews on their T shirts?

How about the flamingos in Florida with pink cement Italians on their lawns?

What do you get when you cross a Pole and a monkey?
Nothing. A monkey's too smart to fuck a Pole.

Did you hear about James Watts' appearance on Julia Child's cooking class?
Giving lessons in how to carve a California condor...

How can you tell if you're overweight?
If you step on your dog's tail and it dies.

Why do crabs have circles under their eyes?
From sleeping in snatches.

Herpes

What's the difference between mono and herpes?
You get mono when you snatch a kiss.

Did you hear about the Polish hooker with herpes?
She charged extra for multiple organisms.

What's the fourth biggest lie?
It's only a cold sore.

Did you hear about the gay guy who was so hip he got Herpes III?

Did you hear about the cure for herpes?
Extra-Strength Tylenol.

What do you call herpes above *and* below the waist?
    Herpes duplex.

What do you get when you fuck a midget?
    Twerpies.
When you fuck a bird?
    Chirpies.
And when you fuck ice cream?
    Slurpies.

What's the difference between love and herpes?
    Herpes is forever.

Lepers

Did you hear about the leper who made his living as a gigolo?

He was doing great until business fell off.

Why was time-out called in the leper hockey game?

There was a face-off in the corner.

How can you tell when a valentine is from a leper?

The tongue's in the envelope.

How could you tell when the poker game between lepers was over?

Someone threw his hand in.

Why did the brothel in the leper colony close down?

The tips weren't worth it.

Know anyone who wants to do charity work in India?

They need people to sort unclaimed feet in the leper colony.

Miscellaneous

A stuck-up fellow comes into a bar and proclaims himself the finest wine connoisseur in the city. He's so good, in fact, that he can identify the vintage and vineyard of any wine they carry, just from a sip.

Skeptical, the barman puts down a glass of white in front of him. "Pinot Grigio from Abruzzi," he proclaims. "1979 was a very poor year; please offer me something better the next time." Next is a rich glass of red. "Mouton Lafitte Rothschild, 1956. From the first row of vines on the westernmost hill. Quite delicious." The man goes on to correctly identify Californian reds, Spanish rosés, and sweet German whites, until the bartender is sick to death of him. Turning aside, he discreetly pees in a glass, chills it, and sets it before the connoisseur.

"Why that's *piss*," he splutters, spitting it on the floor.

"Yeah," says the bartender, "but whose?"

There was a wealthy old gentleman who desired the services of a prostitute, so he arranged with a call-girl service to send over their $1000, top-of-the-line girl. She got all dolled up, rode over to his fancy apartment building, and was escorted up to his penthouse, where the door was opened by the elderly millionaire himself. "And what can I do for you tonight, sir?" she asked in her throatiest voice, dropping her fur coat to reveal a slinky lamé dress.

"Hot tub," he said.

So they went into his luxuriously appointed bathroom where she settled him into the tub. "And now, sir?" she asked.

"Waves," he said.

So she perched herself on the edge of the tub and proceeded to kick her feet vigorously to make waves. "And *next*, sir?"

"Thunder."

Obligingly banging her hand against the side of the tub, she felt it necessary to remind him that he was paying $1000 for her special services, and surely there was some sort of special service she could perform for him.

"Yes," he said, "lightning."

Kicking her feet in the water, banging on the side of the tub with one hand, and flicking the light switch on and off with the other, she felt obliged to give it one more shot. "Sir, you know I am a hooker...Uh, sexual matters are my specialty...Isn't there something along those lines you'd be interested in?"

"In *this* weather?" he said, looking up at her. "Are you crazy?"

Three old guys are sitting around in the park, discussing whose memory goes back the farthest. Says Larry, "I remember being taken to the church, all dressed up in this scratchy white stuff, and having people standing around and someone splashing water on me."

"Aww, that's nothing," says Irv. "I can remember this nice, dark room, and then being squeezed something terrible, and coming out into this big bright room and being spanked—it was awful."

"I got you two beat by a mile," says Fred. "I remember going to a picnic with my father and coming back with my mother."

What's blue and comes in Brownies?
　Cub Scouts.

What's gray and comes in quarts?
　Elephants.

Why do Valley Girls wear two diaphragms?
　Fer shurr, fer shurr.

The Israelites were all waiting anxiously at the foot of the mountain, knowing that Moses had had a tough day negotiating with God over the Commandments. Finally a tired Moses came into sight. "I've got some good news and some bad

news, folks," he said. "The good news is that I got
Him down to ten. The bad news is that adultery's
still in."

You know why sex is like a bridge game?
>You don't need a partner if you have a good
hand.

What's the definition of mixed emotions?
>When you see your mother-in-law backing
off a cliff in your brand new Mercedes.

. Did you hear that Air Florida now serves Key
Largo, Key West... and Key Bridge?
That they've got two new classes besides
smoking and nonsmoking... swimming and non-
swimming?
That they have free drinks on all flights... they
just have to stop and pick up the ice.

Which of the following words is out of place: *wife,
dog, meat, blow job*?
>*Blow job.* You can beat your wife, you can
beat your dog, you can beat your meat, but
nothing beats a blow job.

What do cowboy hats and hemorrhoids have in common?

Sooner or later every asshole has one.

Two little kids, aged six and eight, decide it's time to learn how to swear. So the eight-year-old says to the six-year-old, "Okay, you say 'ass' and I'll say 'hell.'"

All excited about their plan, they troop downstairs, where their mother asks them what they'd like for breakfast. "Aw, hell," says the eight-year-old, "gimme some Cheerios." His mother backhands him off the stool, sending him bawling out of the room, and turns to the younger brother. "What'll you have?"

"I dunno," quavers the six-year-old, "but you can bet your ass it ain't gonna be Cheerios."

How do you get twenty Argentines into a phone booth?

Tell 'em they own it.

What's the difference between erotic and kinky?

Erotic is when you use a feather; kinky is when you use the whole chicken.

Why did Begin besiege Beirut?

To impress Jody Foster.

The newlywed couple is ushered into the doctor's office. The husband is clearly embarrassed by the circumstances, but makes it clear that the visit is his idea. "You see, doctor," he confides, "my wife, she eats like a horse."

"That's absolutely nothing to be concerned about," says the doctor reassuringly. "Many young women have surprisingly hearty appetites."

"Oh I know, doctor," says the young man. "But my wife spends all day on all fours in the barn, and all she'll eat is barley, oats, and hay."

"Hmmm," says the doctor, sitting and thinking quietly for a few minutes. Then he turns and begins scribbling on a piece of paper.

"Can you cure her, doctor?" asks the new husband anxiously. "Is that some sort of prescription?"

"No, no, no," says the doctor. "It's a permit so she can shit in the streets."

A lovelorn young man wrote to an advice columnist as follows:

Dear Abby,

I just met the most terrific girl and we get along fabulously. I think she's the one for me. There's just one problem: I can't remember from our first date if she told me she had T.B. or V.D. What should I do?

—Confused

Abby replies:

Dear Confused,

If she coughs, fuck her.

First guy: "Know how to keep an asshole in suspense?"
Second guy: "No, how?"
First guy: "I'll tell you later."

Why does Dolly Parton have such a small waist?
Nothing grows in the shade.

How can you tell Dolly Parton's kids in the playground?
Stretch marks on their lips.

Did you hear about the eighty-year-old man who streaked the flower show?
He won first prize for his dried arrangement.

How do you get a Kleenex to dance?
Blow a little boogie into it.

Joe: "How many birds in a flock?"
Sam: "I dunno."
Joe: "How many bees in a hive?"
Sam: "I dunno."
Joe: "How many lives does a cat have?"
Sam: "Nine."
Joe: "Well how come if you don't know shit about

the birds and the bees, you know so much about pussy?"

What's the worst thing about being an egg?
> You only get laid once; you only get eaten once; it takes you ten minutes to get hard and three minutes to get soft; you come in a box with eleven other guys; and only your mother sits on your face.

What's the definition of a real buddy?
> Someone who'll go downtown and get two blow jobs, and come back and give you one.

Two guys are walking across the street when they run into a mutual friend, and they comment on how prosperous-looking he is. It turns out he has every reason to be: he's got an eighty-foot yacht, a beautiful wife, a private jet plane, and a million dollars in the bank.

You can imagine their surprise when they run into him two weeks later, dressed in rags and shuffling along dejectedly. They press the sad story out of him. Apparently, he loaned the yacht to a friend who ran it aground and wrecked it, and he had no insurance.

"So?" say the two guys. "It's only a boat."

"Yes, but I didn't have any insurance on the jet either, and it was destroyed in a fire at the airstrip."

"Hey, take heart," say his friends, "at least you've still got your lovely wife and your bank balance."

"Not so fast, fellas," says the poor guy. "My wife ditched me for another guy and her lawyer took me for every cent I had. I'll tell you, if I've learned one thing from all of this, here's what it is: If it flies, floats, or fucks, lease it."

What's the ultimate rejection?

While you're masturbating, your hand falls asleep.

Did you hear about the latest over-the-counter scare?

Someone slipped Krazy Glue into Preparation H.

This really conceited guy is fucking this really conceited girl.

Says she, "Aren't I tight?"

Says he, "No, just full."

Sam Lefkovitz is having an intimate party to celebrate his thirty immensely profitable years in the construction business. "You know," he laments to his friends, "over the years I have constructed dozens of enormous projects in and

107

around this city, but am I known as Sam the Builder? No.

"And over the years I have contributed literally millions of dollars to charitable causes of one sort or another, but am I called Sam the Philanthropist? No, sir.

"But suck *one* little cock…"

What's organic dental floss?

    Pubic hair.

Queen Elizabeth and Lady Di are out for a drive in the royal car on a Sunday afternoon, and they slow down when they see a man by the roadside signaling for help. But no sooner has the car come to a stop than he springs to the door, pulls out a gun, and orders them both out of the car. "Queen Elizabeth," he snarls, "hand over that snazzy diamond tiara you're always wearing."

"I'm terribly sorry, my good man," says the queen, "but I'm afraid I don't wear it on Sundays."

"Aw, hell," says the guy. "Well listen, Di, hand over that fancy engagement ring I keep seeing in all the pictures."

"I'm terribly sorry," says Lady Di sweetly, "but I'm afraid I didn't put it on this morning. It must still be on my night table."

"Aw, shit," growls the guy. "I guess I'll just grab the car." So off he drives at the wheel of the Bentley, leaving the two women walking down the road in the direction of London. After a few minutes have passed, Lady Di asks the queen,

"Pardon my curiosity, Your Highness, but I'm quite sure you had that tiara on this morning. Didn't you?"

"Indeed I did," confesses the queen, blushing slightly and pointing. "I hid it . . . down there. And you, Diana, weren't you wearing your ring?"

Yes she had been, says Diana, turning beet red, and she had resorted to the same hiding place.

They walk a few more steps in companionable silence when Queen Elizabeth lets out a little sigh. "I do wish Princess Margaret had been with us," she says. "We could have saved the Bentley."

Too Tasteless to Be Included in This Book

What do you have when you've got 10,000 blacks at the bottom of the ocean?

A good start.

Why don't their mothers let little black kids play in the sandbox?

Because the cats bury them.

You know how fancy mail-order catalogs offer those ridiculously expensive, exclusive items for sale? In a recent one there was a full-page spread for a $25,000 pair of boots made of human skin.

In fine print, at the bottom, it said, "In black, $7.50."

How do you baby-sit for a black kid?

Wet its lips and stick it to the wall.

How do you get it unstuck?

Teach it to say "motherfucker."

What does a JAP do with her asshole in the morning?

Sends him out to work.

How do you stop five blacks from raping a white girl?

Throw 'em a basketball.

Did you hear about Ronald Reagan's new Kentucky Fried Chicken outlet?

It only serves right wings and assholes.

What do you do with a dead black?

Carve him out and use him for a wet suit.

What's the difference between a mother-in-law and a bucket of shit?

The bucket.

What's yellow on the outside, black on the inside, and goes screaming over a cliff?

A school bus full of black kids.

What's the difference between a JAP and a toilet?
    A toilet doesn't follow you around for months
    after you use it.

Why do women have legs?
    So they don't leave tracks like snails.

How do you save a drowning Puerto Rican?
    You say you don't know? Good.

Would you like to see your favorite tasteless joke(s) in print? If so, send them to:

Blanche Knott
% Ballantine Books
201 East 50th Street
New York, New York 10022

Remember, no compensation or credit can be given, and only those "tasteless" enough will be included!

On the Lighter Side...

TA-49